SUSTAINED TO SERVE

Communion And Offering Prayers

Wava M. Burt

CSS Publishing Company, Inc., Lima, Ohio

SUSTAINED TO SERVE

For more information about CSS Publishing Company resources, visit our website at www.csspub.com or e-mail us at custserv@csspub.com or call (800) 241-4056.

ISBN 0-7880-2303-9   PRINTED IN U.S.A.

This book is dedicated to
Carol Dearing
and other dear friends whose
affirmation and encouragement
led to the printing of these words.

Acknowledgments

I give thanks for Karla Burt Shaffer who has helped put my words into usable form. It is a real joy to work with one who remains my friend as well as my daughter.

I rejoice in being part of a church family that carries me above life's flood, when needed, and trusts enough to share with me. I am thankful for that atmosphere where God can inspire and where together we can gather at the Lord's table. The elder's prayers herein were written at specific times with my specific church family in mind. That family, with God's help, is on every page.

Table Of Contents

Prayers For Offering

Introduction

Perhaps, the most spiritually awakening experience for me thus far in my life has been to serve as an elder at First Christian Church (Disciples of Christ) in Liberal, Kansas. Regardless of the number of terms served, there continues to be a humble awareness of accountability, shepherding of, and ministering to the entire church family.

One of the great and meaningful traditions of the Christian Church (Disciples of Christ) is the observation of the Lord's Supper whenever worshipers meet together. As elders offer prayers at the table, responsibility goes beyond personal needs and becomes that of directing the congregation's spiritual focus upon the elements and intimate remembrance of the ever-present, living Christ. Through prayerful direction, ordinary lives and circumstances are opened to that presence, with freedom to bring whatever we are carrying at the moment to the table.

Each communion prayer in this book includes bread and cup. Prayers of thanksgiving are in celebration of offerings given. They are sprinkled throughout the church year and other seasons and can be modified for various situations.

If there is a message in the pages, I would hope it is in the realization that no special language, no special words need be learned to communicate with God. God meets us where we are, as we are, whether partaking of meals in our homes or around the Lord's table.

In All Seasons

Yes, Lord, we do want to remember you — not as some historical event, but to recall you into the most intimate core of our being.

Help us remain steadfast amidst change — changing seasons of the church, nature, and personal experiences.

Some here today may sense new beginnings blossoming in our lives.
Celebrate with us.

Others feel stifling heat of conflict and discontentment.
Shower those with calming assurance that this, too, will surely pass.

Sustain us with your tender hand of mercy when we are detached, tossed about, and carried from the source of life.

We're not always ready for the snow, Lord.
When quiet coldness blankets us, wrap us in your Spirit.
Warm us with reassurance that you are the constant reality of all seasons.

Give us your peace as we partake of this bread and cup, emblems of your forever presence.

We pray in the name of the anticipated Christ Child. Amen.

Preparation

God of Advent, the excitement and anticipation of Jesus'
coming once again surround us.
Greens are hung and outwardly we seem ready for his arrival.

Even as decorations have been retrieved from closets and
corners, may we re-discover vital inspiration in our lives that
has been put aside for mundane responsibilities.

Help us, O God, to wait patiently as we hope for things
unseen, ever alert to your revealing.

Forgive us, Lord, when we hope for a king and overlook the
infant.

We are reminded by the bread and cup before us of the self-
giving love of Jesus.

By partaking of these emblems, we proclaim our hope in the
Christ who was, is, and always will be — the Christ who died
to give us wholeness and healing. Amen.

Through Hope, Peace, Love, And Joy

Almighty and ever-powerful God, we come to your table humbly remembering your gift to us of your Son, that we might have hope eternally.

Forgive us, O God, when we get so busy with ourselves that we overlook the wonder of Christ's birth.

Bless us, Lord, as we consume these emblems. May our eyes be opened to see you more clearly and our faith renewed.

May we know your divine presence in and around us as we partake.

In Jesus' name we pray. Amen.

Anticipation

Lord of Steadfast Love, we are thankful to be yours. Forgive us when personal desire or pettiness obscures loving mercy and grace meant to be ours.

This Advent season we anticipate Christ's coming, and anticipate new beginnings. We have prepared bread and wine, symbols of your great sacrifice for us, and we remember.

Call us by name, Lord, as we partake. Remind each one of your mission for us and that new life can triumph, as shown in both Christ's birth and resurrection.

We seek you at the manger. We seek you at the table, Lord.

May we allow fresh innocence of the Christ Child to mature in us, deepening understanding and acceptance of each other and stimulating our yearning to be servants in your Realm.

We pray in the name of your Son, our Christ. Amen.

Room To Remember?

Everlasting Parent God, who revealed yourself through the Holy Child born at Bethlehem, our hearts are filled with joy in these anniversary days of his birth.

If our lives have been crowded with other things so that we turn away as he was turned away from the inn in Bethlehem, forgive us, we pray.

Though we may not have expensive gifts to bring, we offer a life lived in his name.

As we break the bread and hold the cup in memory of our Lord Jesus Christ, bless us in our dedication to his service.

May we see others as your children and as our brothers and sisters.

At this Christmas season as we remember your great gift to us, accept our lives as gifts to you in this hour of communion.

In the name of Jesus the Christ, we pray. Amen.

Crown Or Cradle

Source of Strength and Salvation, may we recognize you in all things and may we be ready to receive you, whether you come in a kingly fashion or as a crying baby.

Lord, we offer these gifts as symbols of that readiness and pray for the guidance of your Great Spirit in the ways they are used.

In the name of Christ Jesus we pray. Amen.

After They All Go Home

Gracious Provider of all good things, we are beginning to relax a bit after the intensity of preparation.

Gifts have been opened, empty boxes and crumpled wrapping paper are in trash containers, and lingering strains of Christmas carols hesitantly drift past as if wondering whether they should be here.

Images of the season color our days — faces joyful upon reunion; fragrance of simmering coffee, turkey, and sweet potatoes; conversations and laughter; tears of departure.

For some, these days have been a stinging reminder that a loved one who celebrated last year's season is not here. Others rejoice in the embrace of one who was not expected to be with us now, but is.

Lord God, we have given and we have received.

Our prayer is that preparation for others has instilled in us that preparation for you is ongoing.

We thank you, God, for sending your Son and ask your blessing upon the offerings before us.

We pray in the name of the Christmas Babe, the Christ. Amen.

Security For The Wild Ride

God of everything old and everything new, we praise you as we anticipate a new year, so fresh and new, like the Christmas Babe, needing our care.

Lord, we at times feel like we are on a roller coaster of hours, days, and years with everything passing so swiftly that we are unable to grasp and hold even those seconds dearest to us.

Forgive us, God, when we lose sight of you in the blur of life's ride.

As we partake of these emblems, we recall you into our most intimate selves and may we hold for a moment the comfort of your closeness.

May we not be lost ineffectively in days past, but take your hand, Lord, to move joyfully into days ahead with the security of your presence.

We thank you, God, for our lives and the life of your Son, Jesus Christ, in whose name we pray. Amen.

In A Wonderland

God of Beauty and Love, we admire your handiwork as the cleansing, purifying snow covers the land. We thank you for all our senses with which to enjoy the brightness, the sounds and smells of winter, the warmth of our homes, and a friend's touch.

Forgive us, Lord, when we fail to see you in all that is around us.

At this table, we especially thank you for your Son, Jesus Christ.

Warm our hearts with receptiveness for all your children as we partake of these symbols of your absolute acceptance of us.

By recalling Jesus into the centers of our beings, may we be shown insights into personal problems and strengthened to serve you more eagerly.

In Christ's name we pray. Amen.

In Days Fulfilled

Eternal, ageless God, you give us days to live.
We aimlessly turn calendar pages, mistakenly assuming that our lives are complete if written entries cram each space.

You faithfully turn insignificant tasks into life's blessings. We often miss those blessings as we clamor to work through lists of chores.

Lord, make us aware of moments provided.
May we cling to each blessing and be inspired to share all you have given, even ourselves.

Bless the offerings, O God, and those who have given them. We pray in the name of Christ, who gave all for us. Amen.

Through Riches Provided

Divine Source of the good we enjoy, you have handed us a Christmas gift and watched as we unwrapped it to discover the newborn Savior.

We cherish your gift and the fact that you gave it.

Now, we wish to highlight the beauty of this treasure received and tell its story to others.

May our offerings today implement such display and sharing.

We pray in the name of the One given to us all. Amen.

With Proclamation And Abiding Love

O God of Light and Love, we come before you remembering him who was proclaimed king on that first Palm Sunday.

We would make him king of all things in our lives as we partake of this loaf and cup in witness of our loyalty to him.

We renew our pledge to serve him by determining to serve one another.

May we not join the crowd which crowned him and then crucified him.

Let our lives be a constant confession of abiding allegiance to Jesus, the Christ, in whose name we pray. Amen.

As We Watch And Wait

Eternal Source of Peace, calm our uneasiness about the coming sacrifice as we join you at this table. Unlike your disciples on this night, we know about Good Friday.

It's not always comfortable knowing the extreme price you paid. How could we possibly be worthy?

In our recognition that pain and suffering are no strangers to you, we realize, too, how very closely you share our agonies. Through any possible despair, help us focus on the resurrection, not the suffering.

Forgive us, Lord, when, like your disciples, we are slow to understand and cannot watch with you one hour.

We accept your sacrifice. Come to us, stay with us, we need you here, breaking this bread, drinking this cup.

May we be centered on the risen Christ, in whose name we pray. Amen.

Not Fearing, For He Is Risen

God of Resurrecting Life, your never-ending love is beyond our comprehension.

We are humbled that you would sacrifice your Son for us. We are in awe of and thankful for your plan for his resurrection and ours.

Forgive us, Lord, when we take it so for granted.

Be present, O Holy Spirit, as we partake of these symbols, witnessing our loyalty to him. May we experience renewal of life within us as we recall our resurrected Christ.

Let us be filled with the excitement of the resurrection.

Christ is risen! Thank you, God. Amen.

Released To Hope

Ever-living God, we need your resurrection. We are so grateful for the life you have given us and are reminded that it is fragile.

Tragic accidents claim some while another may fall at the violent hand of one who wishes to do harm.

Lord, you walked willfully to Golgotha. How could we ever doubt your vision of hope through despair?

Forgive us, Lord, when we fail to recognize you. And, in the radiance of Easter light, reveal yourself to us now as we partake of the bread and cup, symbols of your total sacrifice and life anew.

Roll away the stones of hardened hearts or hopelessness that would entomb us.

May we be free in you, O Christ, and in your name we pray. Amen.

After Tarrying At The Tomb

O victorious Holy One, you know our need to flee in disarray from situations that confuse us and cause us pain.

May we not run in fright and frenzy, O Lord. Instead, may our searching keep us at the tomb until your appearance prepares us to share the proclamation that you are alive!

Call us each by name that we might know you.

Fill us with the bread you broke and the cup you poured.

May we tarry at this table to be nourished and invigorated, then hurry from here to tell everyone that we have seen you, O risen Christ. Amen.

(John 20:11-18)

With Hope

Almighty Source of Hope, accept the gifts we offer.

We sometimes see ourselves as small and struggling.
Remind us, O God, that we are Easter people, your people,
people of hope!

Dream with us, Lord, about possibilities, about what you
want to happen.

You so loved the world that you gave your only Son.

Gently lead us to become more like you in your generosity.

Amen.

By Each New Invitation

Loving Creator, we are awed by your universal magnitude when we survey star-filled skies, observe the dawning of a new day, or absorb rays of the spring sun.

We are aware of your very personal touch when hearing the tiniest bird's song and when emotions swell within us, remembering that you, too, have experienced frustration, despair, sorrow, and joy through Jesus, your sacrificial gift.

Let us see in this common act of communion what it means truly to share as your family and be part of the Body of Christ. As we partake of the bread and cup, may we be strengthened as with life-sustaining food and may our hearts be quieted by conversing with you.

Lord, let us be reminded that Christ and the invitation to commune are constant and everlasting, just as each day brings a new dawn.

May we see with new eyes your love and glory in our midst.

We pray in the name of Jesus Christ. Amen.

Even On April 15

Generous Provider of all good gifts, these days when we're hearing so much about taxes, we are reminded of Jesus' words, "Render unto Caesar the things that are Caesar's and unto God the things that are God's."

Help us, O God, distinguish the difference between yours and Caesar's.

Help us focus on you, both when we feel divided and when we feel whole.

We thank you for the ability to work and earn, and we offer these gifts to show our desire to further your Realm in a material world.

In Jesus' name we pray. Amen.

Thankful For Mothers

Almighty God, who, like a mother cares for us ungrudgingly and sacrificially, we thank you, especially today for mothers who showed us ways to share early in life.

Make vivid the memories of those examples and reassure us now, as individuals and as a church family, that giving of ourselves never deducts, but adds to our wealth as your children and strengthens our bond in the Body of Christ.

Bless the givers and the gifts, O God. We pray in the name of Jesus, your given Son. Amen.

Refreshed

Almighty God, who as a father enfolds us with strength and wisdom, and provides for us untiringly, we come to this table intimately sensing your presence.

When we seem to be crossing endless sands of stress and despair, you are the oasis we seek. May mirages of idleness, complacency, and self-serving not divert our paths. But, may our direction be straight as you call us into your care.

O Lord, may we be refreshed and renewed as we rest totally in you partaking of this bread and cup, the symbols of your saving grace and sacrificial love for us.

In Jesus' name we pray. Amen.

In Harvest

Rumbling engines break the silence of dawn and remind us that golden grain is ripe for reaping and will not wait.

May we not slumber through opportunities to gather the many blessings you give us, O Lord.

Grant us strength for the harvest.

May warehouses be in constant readiness, not as places to hoard the crop, but where goodness is nurtured and matured for scattering upon a world hungry for your feast.

Thank you, thank you, God. Amen.

With Warmth

Loving, giving God, we return a portion of our financial blessings for the work of your Realm.

Remind us, O God, that you are a part of jobs that provide income, part of the love we feel from friends and family, and part of the warming summer sun. For these things and more, we are grateful.

You are among us here and we ask that you preside with congregation leaders as decisions are made how best to utilize these gifts.

May our church home grow as a haven of hope and healing for your children.

In Christ's name we pray. Amen.

Cleansed

Ever-present, sustaining God, we come as your family to
share a meal.
We praise you for wonders not fully understood.
We're surprised by harsh, bold thunder and quieted by soft
raindrops, which gather together to create rushing rivers.

Rain on *us* now, Lord. Cleanse us of uncertainties and
indecision. Soothe the sting of conflict and emptiness of loss.
May we inhale freshness of acceptance and unconditional
love.
Quench egotistical struggles with the knowledge that each of
us is so uniquely valuable to you.

As we partake of these emblems, may we be drenched in the
recollection of Jesus' life, death, and resurrection.
Gather us, also, Lord, that together we might become streams
of service, forgiveness, and truth.

We pray in the name of Christ who offers eternal, life-giving
water to all. Amen.

Celebrating Freedom

We have seen the rockets' red glare, O God.

Help us, we pray, to influence the world positively so that bombs will never burst as a means of hurting any of your dear children.

The bread and cup before us are reminders that you, O Christ, have set us free.

Help us to stand firm against submission to any yoke of slavery.

And, may we never seek to put that yoke on another, whether out of racism, in a corporation, in relationships, or in the name of religion.

Help us, God, not to use freedom as opportunities for self-indulgence.

But, rather, may we serve one another in love at this table and in all of life, following your example of sacrificial deliverance.

We remember you now, O liberating Christ, and pray in your name. Amen.

(Galatians 5:1, 13)

Independence

God of all nations, we thank you for freedom. Remind us, Lord, that alongside any freedom is responsibility.

When we choose, may it be wisely; when we speak, may it be an expression to build relationships.

May we assemble to worship and praise, never to condemn or destroy.

May the arms we bear be the sword of the Spirit as we are shielded by faith.

May we never seek independence from you, O God, but depend on you for strength, courage, and guidance.

This bread and cup symbolize your great sacrifice for us. Our partaking symbolizes our allegiance to you.

We realize we can only truly be free by your grace and the salvation of Jesus, the Christ, in whose name we pray. Amen.

Free To Give

God of Love, Protection, and Guidance, our prayer before you is one of thanksgiving and hope this day.

Strengthen us and show us the way to use these gifts we offer to develop peace and righteousness, that we might have true freedom.

Help us cheerfully accept our share of responsibility to make this a better world after the example of Jesus Christ, in whose name we pray. Amen.

From Tears To Victory

Ever-present, living, loving God, we adore you. We lay before you on this table experiences of the week just past.

We have been blessed by a peaceful, renewing holiday with loved ones, we have been inspired by words of your global ministry; and united, we cry for loss of youth and grieve the passing of aged wisdom.

We recall now, Lord, that Jesus first broke bread and poured wine to help prepare friends for his premature death, then triumphed victoriously over that death with resurrection and life.

Restore to us, now, the joy of our salvation, so vividly depicted in these emblems of bread and wine.

Enrich us with your grace, instill us with desire, that we may be compelled to bring about good.

You have shown us the way, O God. We now remember the teacher, our Savior, Jesus Christ, in whose name we pray. Amen.

Colored With Closeness

Master Painter, Designer, we praise you and rejoice in the beauty with which you surround us.

You provide us with landscapes from which we eagerly grasp vivid fall colors and apprehensively anticipate a winter that now only peeks at us before retreating.

You provide us, too, O God, with the portrait of one who triumphed over death's cold darkness.

As we partake of the bread and cup, representing the broken body and blood of Jesus Christ, we ask that you replace our doubt with touches of courage and shining hope.

And, if a winter of desolation should catch us unaware or linger longer than expected, Lord, may we be sustained by the bright assurance of your constant closeness.

We pray in the name of the risen Savior. Amen.

Giving In Return

Loving and giving God, there are so many pleasurable things surrounding us this fall season and we thank you.

Lord, help our senses peak to where we notice and experience each sight, sound, and sensation every day.

Our offerings symbolize the need and desire to share ourselves in return for your immeasurable gifts to us. Help us to be more aware of sharing not only our money, but our time, talents, and love for all your children.

May we in some way extend your peace and comfort by our giving. In Christ's name we pray. Amen.

A Shopping God

Almighty Giver of Good, we would feel humbled imagining
your going to the mall to find the perfect gift for us.

Yet, that's what you've done when we, seeking, open the
Bible to find perfect words of encouragement.

That is what you've done when color has faded from our lives
and a fluttering autumn leaf reminds us that we need not feel
dormant, but vivid.

You have shopped for us, Lord, when an inspired friend
confronts us with new images of you.

And, we find our name on the perfect gift when, feeling like
life's lights have been extinguished, we are illumined by a
myriad of lingering stars in the air of a crisp autumn dawn.

May we hold your precious gifts dear, O God, and may we
share offerings brought today with the same undemanding
love as that with which you have blessed us.

We pray in the name of Jesus Christ, your most sacrificial gift.
Amen.

Meeting And Remembering

Redeeming God, Creator of all, we thank you for this day and the joy of this fellowship.

We especially thank you for the sacrifice of your Son, Jesus Christ.

As we meet at this table, we remember him, his life, and his ministry.

Cleanse our hearts, O God, and awake in us a renewed spirit and desire for your guidance.

May we be messengers of your love and light to all people.

In Christ's name we pray. Amen.

Giving Unlimited

Giving God, we acknowledge our many blessings and realize your potential to give is far greater than we can imagine.

We are confronted, both personally and as a church, with financial decisions — how to cover costs of things we believe to be necessities and wanting more of what we know are not necessities.

We ask you, Lord, for guidance and insights to best use our resources and for forgiveness when we embrace selfishness.

We bring tithes and offerings not as a public display of what we have, but as a symbol of what we are willing to share.

You hold nothing back from us, God, and may we, created in your image, reach for our giving potential.

We pray in the name of Jesus Christ, your ultimate gift. Amen.

When Times Are Tough

Source of All Blessings, we offer ourselves, including our money, to you.

We return these offerings to you through the channels of your church.

Lord, watch over our giving, our use of the gifts, and our acceptance of how amounts given affect our activities and comfort here in your house, also.

May we deal with that reality in maturity and love such as that with which you would deal with us.

We pray in the name of Jesus Christ, giver of salvation. Amen.

Bringing Everything To The Table

Divine God, who receives us as we are, we accept your invitation to surround your table, bringing many things.

We now give to you any tension of jobs left undone, senses of loss in our lives, and concerns about death or pain.

Share with us, too, joy and laughter.

We're uneasy knowing there are those who wish to terrorize and we are anguished for victims of such acts.

As we partake of the bread and cup, remind us that you, too, carried a heavy load to the cross and now in victory beyond, you carry for us whatever we are willing to leave here.

Help us rearrange fragmented feelings into a collage of hope, direction, and discovery.

Rid us of anything that would separate us from you and create in us clean hearts, O God.

We pray in the name of Christ Jesus, for whom we are so thankful. Amen.

Setting Priorities

Loving Lord, we put so much time and energy into acquiring and preserving material possessions, things that can so quickly be destroyed.

Yet, when they are gone, the sun still rises, seasons change, flowers continue blooming, friends' laughter renews us, and life breathes within us.

Essential things are not seen by our eyes, nor are they in our control.

You, Lord, are our strength; you sustain us.

We pray that our focus on you and your sovereignty, O God, will free us to share all you have given us.

Bless these gifts and the givers to your service.

In Christ's name we pray. Amen.

But, Don't Forget Your Luggage

Accepting God of Love, we, your people, bring many things to your table — uncertainties, despair, conflict in relationships, conflict of our will and your will, pain of loss, and joy of new beginnings.

We are amazed that you want us with whatever baggage we carry, but, we are here.

As we partake of this bread and cup, remind us that Jesus experienced all the feelings that we do, including despair and the ecstasy of resolve through resurrection.

We accept the sacrifice of your Son and these emblems in remembrance.
Although we find it difficult to understand your unconditional grace, we offer ourselves to you.
Hold us, embrace us, assure us.

We pray in the name of our Christ. Amen.

Awakened To Give

Eternal Source of Blessing, may we, with these gifts, make a difference for Christ in our community and world.

May we know the strength, joy, and peace of surrender, the love and fellowship from each other, and the happy experience of worship that we share here.

We want to have an awakened faith, and we know this family will become increasingly great as we rejoice in our giving.

Thankfully we pray in Jesus' name. Amen.

Loved And Amazed

Almighty Source of Love and Life, we praise you.

We are at this table to remember the life, death, and resurrection of Jesus.

We remember, too, the memory verse learned so early in childhood, "God is love."
Then, surely, love is God.

Is it possible, Lord, that the pacifying warmth I feel when reading a message from a faraway friend is you?

And, if I should share something for a starving stranger's meal or open my door to a troubled friend, could that possibly be you, too?

It seems like such a small thing, considering what you sacrificed for us.
We hold that sacrifice in full view as we partake of the bread and the wine.

Forgive us, Lord, when our amazement that you could live through us directs us toward the magnificent and past the obvious opportunities.

May we willingly receive you, then easily and openly release your love to others. Amen.

Reaping The Sown

Gracious and glorious God, you have given us life and everything necessary to sustain it.

Forgive us, Lord, when we anticipate harvest without planting.

Have mercy when we envision full warehouses without imagining toil.

Weed from our hearts attitudes that selfishly blind us from the glare of others' needs.

And, cultivate us with vision and passion to see ways of sharing our plenty so our community and world might know the joy and peace of your love.

Lord, receive our offerings and adoration.

We pray in Christ's name. Amen.

God's Management With Ease

Sovereign God of Order and Love, forgive us when we behave as though *we* are all powerful.

We at times feel scattered and frazzled as we deal with daily demands, O Lord, yet, you run a whole universe from meteors to microorganisms with relative ease.

Recognize our needs, O God, and remind us in the calm of these moments that we need not bear the weight of our worlds alone.

Grant us your quieting strength as we partake of the bread and cup which symbolize Jesus' death and resurrection.

O God, we accept your grace.

We seek your support and direction in our lives as we remember with grateful hearts Jesus, the Christ, in whose name we pray. Amen.

No Other Gods?

Covenanting God of Abraham and Moses, you are the Lord our God and we shall have no other gods before you.

God of Creation, we are in your image, yet somehow imagine that material things accumulated make us what we are.

You are the Balm of Gilead, but we go shopping to feel better.

You are the Rock of Ages, but our trust is in the stock market.[1]

Everlasting Provider, you give us life's meaning in family time, quality relationships, time at church, time to volunteer.

Forgive us when those things are pushed aside for corporate enslavement as we idolize mammon.[2]

We ask your help in putting aside rival gods as we present these offerings.

May we be reminded not to use people and worship things, but to use things and value people.

May our faith be in you, Jehovah. We pray in the name of the Son you sent us, O God of salvation. Amen.

---

1. Inspired by the choir anthem, *He Is Jehovah*, Betty Jean Robinson, arr. by Gary Rhodes, copyright 1982 and arrangement copyright 1985. Jehovah-Jireh Music/ASCP.

2. Thoughts from "A Conversation with Jim Wallis," *ALIVE NOW* January/February, 1997.

When Available Funds Dwindle

Source of All Blessing, we offer ourselves, including our money, by returning offerings to you through the channels of your church.

Lord, watch over our giving and use of the gifts. Keep us alert to the knowledge of how the amount we give affects potential ministries for you, as well as our comfort here in this, your church.

May we deal with that reality in maturity and love such as that with which you deal with us.

We pray in the name of Jesus Christ, giver of salvation. Amen.

Impact Of Giving

O God, we have observed how badly the world needs what Christ can give.

Our gifts this morning express our strong feeling that we need to seek to make an impact for truth and life.

We ask that you accept our giving, in Jesus' name. Amen.

Gratefully Remembering

Eternal God and Creator of us all, we come before you in this sacred hour of communion with gratitude.

We partake of these emblems with grateful remembrance of your Son, of his perfect life, and of his death on the cross.

May we examine our hearts, striving to be worthy followers of him.

Give us the willingness and courage to serve you and the love to be forgiving.

Speak to us at this, your table, that we may have life abundantly through Jesus Christ our Lord, in whose name we pray. Amen.

No Dues Necessary

Gracious friend God, no payment is required to enter your house.
But, at your invitation, we've been received as guests.

We've at times been amused, we've been diverted from outside stresses and demands, and we cherish memories of times together here.

Lord, you have presented yourself to us wholly without restraint, yet you give us the *option* of presenting offerings to you.

Forgive us, Lord, when we see these moments as a routine intermission.
Help us grasp within us this expression which is, indeed, a deepening strengthening part of our worship.

Accept money offered and accept us, O God, for we want to live for you in service of yours even as Christ sacrificed for us.
Amen.

Refueled

We thank you, O God, for this table to which we come, recalling our Lord whose body was broken and whose blood was shed that we might have life.

We are grateful that we can leave the turmoil of the past week and gather here to gain strength for the days ahead.

Let the emblems speak to us of redemption from sin and life eternal which we know through him whose life, death, and resurrection are represented here.

Give us strength to face temptation, courage to meet adversities, and forgiveness for our failures.

May we always be mindful of your goodness. In Jesus' name we pray. Amen.

Yearning To Care

O God, Source of all that we have and are, we praise you.

We, at this moment, reflect on the many good things in our lives.

Help us not push out of our hearing the cries of the hungry and lonely.
But, instead, let us feel a yearning to love and care for all your people.

Offering our monetary gifts is one way we express our desire to share.
Please accept these gifts, O Lord.

We pray in Christ's name. Amen.

Companion God

O God, we are reverent and humble as we come to this communion table.

We recognize our need for you in all our days and seek your mercy and grace.

We pray that we may ever be humble in your sight and obedient to your directing our lives.

Cleanse our hearts as we prepare to eat this bread and drink this cup which are symbols of Jesus' giving, even unto death.

Help us know a companionship with you that we may truly honor your name which is above every name.

Forgive our unrighteousness and let your joy and peace be with us always.

In the name of Christ, our Lord, we pray. Amen.

Setting Investment Priorities

Ever-present Holy One, we expect you always to be near
when we call upon you.
May we be sensitive to the importance of keeping Sabbath —
some part of our week for you.[1]

We are surrounded with your gifts — nature, air to breathe,
sunshine to warm, rain to replenish, health, and the capacity
to love and be loved.

May we be sensitive to the importance of giving, not the
leftovers, but the cream of the crop, to you in this time of
worship, so that your importance will be reflected in our lives.

We pray in Christ's name. Amen.

---

1. Kim Martin Sadler, Editor, *The Book of Daily Prayer*, United Church
   Press, p. 152.

God's Roving Care

Almighty Source of Thought and Emotion, forgive us when we seek to limit you to our personal concepts of what you should be.

We don't easily comprehend a love with no boundaries. Sustain us with the assurance that we can never be outside your care.

Come to us now; stay with us.
We need you here as we partake of this bread and cup, the emblems of your greatest sacrifice for us.

We receive you, Lord, and thank you for limitless salvation. May the vision of the Living Christ remove any fear of sharing, and may we open ourselves to be instruments of your love.

We pray in the name of Jesus, the Christ. Amen.

Blinded By Sights

Eternal Source of Inspiration, you sometimes place things in our line of vision that we don't really want to see.

We wonder how we can lift up enough joy to offset the pain you share with so many of your children.

We lift up to you this day these offerings, symbols of our dedication to your service, knowing that all the world's misery cannot be relieved, but believing, with your help, O God, that someone's hurt can be healed.

We pray for your presence with those who have given, with those who will make decisions about the use of the gifts, and with those whose needs might be lessened.

Reveal your way to us and use us now, Lord.
We pray in the name of Jesus Christ, who gave all. Amen.

Thankfully Receiving And Serving

O God, who are perfect love, we meet you at this table
wanting to know you better and love you more.

We recognize your majesty, yet sense your intimate touch,
and although we don't understand how or why, we know you
are truly with us and in us.

Help us by faith to accept your grace and in your loving
embrace this moment, may scattered lives be re-centered.

We *receive* this bread and cup, symbols of Christ's broken
body, realizing the loaf is useless if never broken.

We receive, too, your grace.

We *give thanks.*

And, just as the bread is *broken*, we open ourselves to go forth
and *serve.*

As we receive your unconditional love, may we be willing to
extend that same undemanding openness to others, even the
unlovable.

We pray in the name of Christ Jesus. Amen.

Privileged And Committed

God, our friend and confidant, we thank you for the privilege of giving.

We thank you for your generosity in meeting our needs.

Touch our lives as we commit ourselves as your stewards.

Accept these, our gifts, given for the furthering of your Realm.

In Jesus' name we pray. Amen.

Invitation Accepted

O Divine One who is forever near, as we remember you, help us recall, too, that this is your table, that the invitation is yours.

Forgive us our sins, O Lord, and remind us of our blessings.

You have given us daily bread, yet some starve for your goodness and mercy.
Teach us to nourish others as you nourish us.

As we partake of these emblems, knead into our hearts truth and righteousness.
Leaven us with faith, peace, and encouragement that we might rise to heights of service in your name.

And, God, may thirsty ones never have to search for a vessel from which to drink.
Fill us, Lord, with your light and beauty, flavored with willingness to be poured out for a world in need of refreshing.

We pray in the name of the saving, risen Christ. Amen.

www.ingramcontent.com/pod-product-compliance
Lightning Source LLC
Chambersburg PA
CBHW071023040426

42443CB00007B/908